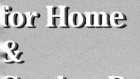

Tips for Tiles

- Cut tiles to a specific shape with craft scissors when necessary.
- To fit tiles in any design, glue tiles around the outside of the design, then glue tiles in the center.
- Remove excess silicone glue with a craft knife.
- Clean finished pieces with window cleaner.
- Do not use finished pieces for hot plates.

Tips for Grout

- When mixing grout, leave a small amount in the bag to use if the mixture needs thickening.
- Mix grout in a plastic container that can be discarded when finished.
- NEVER pour grout down the drain.
- Clean grout from mosaic pieces with baby wipes or a damp sponge.
- Let project dry overnight then clean the surface with window cleaner.
- Mix grout to the consistency of soft putty.

Garden Decor

Clay Pots   pg. 4

Birdhouse   pg. 5

Mailbox   pg. 7

Birdbath   pg. 8-9

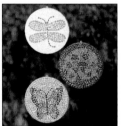
Stepping Stone pg. 10-11

Fountain   pg. 12

Bird Feeder   pg. 13

Table Top   pg. 14-15

Home Decor

Sun Catchers pg. 16-19

Vase & Votive   pg. 20

Window Hanging   pg. 21

Clock   pg. 22

Table Set   pg. 23

Fruit Tray   pg. 24-25

Canisters   pg. 26

Fish Bowl   pg. 27

Folding Screen   pg. 28-29

Sea Life Vase   pg. 30-31

Chest   pg. 32-33

Lamp & Turtle   pg. 34-35

Plant some ivy in this special pot. It will thrive in its colorful little home.

A small flowerpot becomes a work of art when it is covered with glowing mosaics.

Violet Flowerpot

by Lorraine Kazan

THE BEADERY® MATERIALS:
• 1 package each of Alabaster, Light Violet and Violet mosaic pieces • Package of Ivory grout
MATERIALS:
6" x 5½" clay pot • Silicone sealer
DIRECTIONS:
Place Alabaster tiles around pot rim, and randomly place remaining tiles around body of pot.

Floral Flowerpot *(pattern on page 6)*

by Lorraine Kazan

THE BEADERY® MATERIALS:
• 1 package each of Jade, Violet, and Alabaster mosaic pieces
• Package of Pewter grout
MATERIALS:
3½" clay flowerpot • Silicone sealer • Ivory grout
DIRECTIONS:
Using pattern, "scatter" flowers around body of pot, use Violet tiles around rim and randomly place remaining tiles around body of pot.

A butterfly and dragonfly stop to rest on the roof of this cool, blue birdhouse.

Birdhouse *(patterns on page 6)*

by Lorraine Kazan

THE BEADERY® MATERIALS:
• 1 package each of Alabaster, Violet, Jade, Cobalt, Tortoise and Light Tiger Coral mosaic pieces • 2 packages of Teal and Light Teal • Package of Pewter grout

MATERIALS:
9" x 6" wood birdhouse • Silicone sealer

DIRECTIONS:
Using pattern, arrange Alabaster tiles around sides of birdhouse. Use Jade tiles around base. Randomly place remaining tiles using picture as guide.

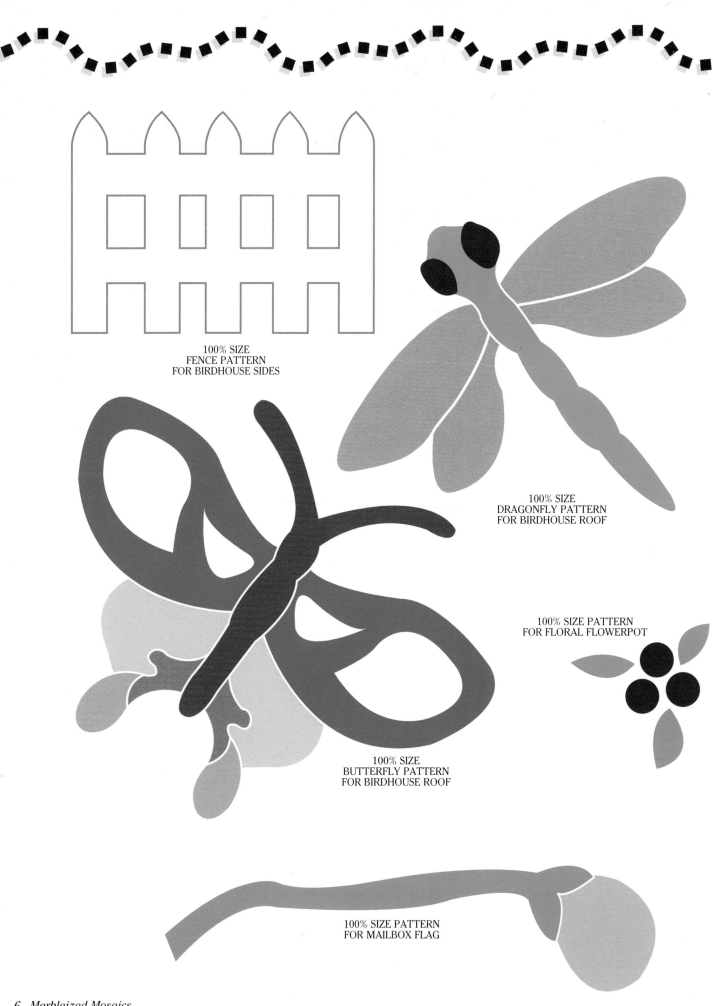

100% SIZE
FENCE PATTERN
FOR BIRDHOUSE SIDES

100% SIZE
DRAGONFLY PATTERN
FOR BIRDHOUSE ROOF

100% SIZE PATTERN
FOR FLORAL FLOWERPOT

100% SIZE
BUTTERFLY PATTERN
FOR BIRDHOUSE ROOF

100% SIZE PATTERN
FOR MAILBOX FLAG

Cover a wood mailbox with dragonfly and flower mosaics for a touch of eternal spring.

Mailbox

by Lorraine Kazan

THE BEADERY® MATERIALS:
• 3 packages of Alabaster • One package each of Violet, Tiger Coral, Teal, Light Tiger Coral, and Jade • 2 packages of White grout
MATERIALS:
Wood mailbox • Silicone sealer

50% SIZE PATTERN
FOR MAILBOX DOOR
(ENLARGE 200%)

50% SIZE PATTERN
FOR MAILBOX SIDES
(ENLARGE 200%)

Marbleized Mosaics 7

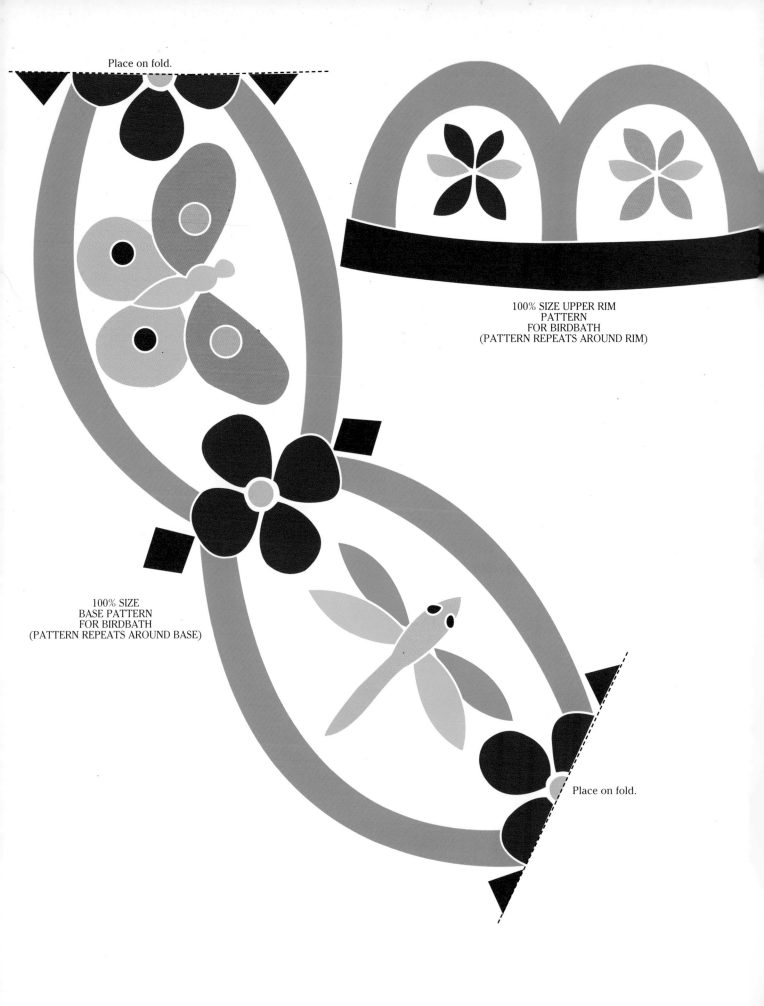

Place on fold.

100% SIZE UPPER RIM
PATTERN
FOR BIRDBATH
(PATTERN REPEATS AROUND RIM)

100% SIZE
BASE PATTERN
FOR BIRDBATH
(PATTERN REPEATS AROUND BASE)

Place on fold.

A birdbath, covered with brilliant flowers, gleams on an Alabaster column.

Birdbath
by Heather McDonald

THE BEADERY® MATERIALS:
• 6 packages of Alabaster • 3 packages of Teal • 2 packages each of Jade and Violet • One package each of Light Rose, Rose, Light Violet, Tiger Coral, Light Teal and Light Tiger Coral • 3 packages of Pewter grout
MATERIALS:
Plastic birdbath • Silicone sealer

Brighten your pathway with a circle of color. Your steps will be as light as the flight of a butterfly.

Butterfly Stepping Stone

by Heather McDonald

THE BEADERY® MATERIALS:
• 1 package each of Light Tiger Coral, Violet, Alabaster, Rose, Light Violet, Light Rose, Light Teal, Teal and Jade mosaic pieces • Package of Pewter grout

MATERIALS:
11" round cement stepping stone • Silicone sealer

DIRECTIONS:
Use pattern for color placement of tiles. Add accent tiles to wings as shown in picture.

Note: Store stepping stones inside during cold weather.

Place on fold.

This water fountain is sure to make a hot day cooler and bring hours of sparkling pleasure.

100% SIZE PATTERN
FOR FOUNTAIN

Fountain

by Janie Ray

THE BEADERY® MATERIALS:
• 1 package each of Cobalt, Teal, Light Teal, Tiger Coral and Light Tiger Coral mosaic pieces • Package of Terra-cotta grout

MATERIALS:
6" clay pot • 6" clay saucer • 12½" x 5" clay bowl • Water pump • Silicone sealer

DIRECTIONS:
Follow picture for placement of patterns.

Dragonflies flitter, irises bloom and fish swim in this delightfully designed birdbath. Everyone will love the whimsy.

50% SIZE PATTERNS
FOR BIRDBATH
(ENLARGE 200%)

Birdbath or Candy Dish

by Lorraine Kazan

THE BEADERY® MATERIALS:
• 1 package each of Alabaster, Teal, Violet, Jade, Light Teal, Tiger Coral and Light Tiger Coral mosaic pieces
• Package of Ivory grout

MATERIALS:
6" x 5½" clay pot • 7½" clay saucer • Silicone sealer

DIRECTIONS:
Follow picture for placement of patterns.

Dragonflies flitter across the top of a table where spring lives all year long.

Dragonfly Table Top

by Mimi Huszer Fagnant

THE BEADERY® MATERIALS:
• 1 package each of Light Rose, Rose, Jade, Tiger Coral and Light Tiger Coral mosaic pieces
• 2 packages of Alabaster mosaic pieces • Package of Ivory grout
MATERIALS:
Wrought iron table with 10" square top • 10" square of plexiglass
• Silicone sealer
DIRECTIONS:
Fill background with Alabaster tiles.

100% SIZE PATTERN
FOR TABLE TOP

Bring the great outdoors inside with this brilliant display of winged dragonflies. It will bring a breath of fresh air to city rooms or country settings.

A gecko curls around colored stones in a wealth of color. Nature has never been more beautiful.

The sun sparkles through this butterfly suncatcher with the look of stained glass...and color dances throughout your room.

SunCatchers
by Barbara Curley Burnett

Dragonfly
THE BEADERY® MATERIALS:
• 1 package each of Light Tiger Coral, Jade and Alabaster mosaic pieces • Package of Ivory grout
MATERIALS:
10" Gallery Glass beveled round blank • Silicone sealer

Gecko
THE BEADERY® MATERIALS:
• 1 package each of Cobalt, Teal, Light Teal, Tiger Coral and Light Tiger Coral mosaic pieces • Package of Pewter grout
MATERIALS:
10" Gallery Glass beveled round blank • Silicone sealer

Butterfly
THE BEADERY® MATERIALS:
• 1 package each of Violet, Rose, Teal, Light Teal and Light Tiger Coral mosaic pieces • Package of Ivory grout
MATERIALS:
10" Gallery Glass beveled round blank • Silicone sealer

Gecko and Butterfly SunCatcher patterns on pages 18-19.

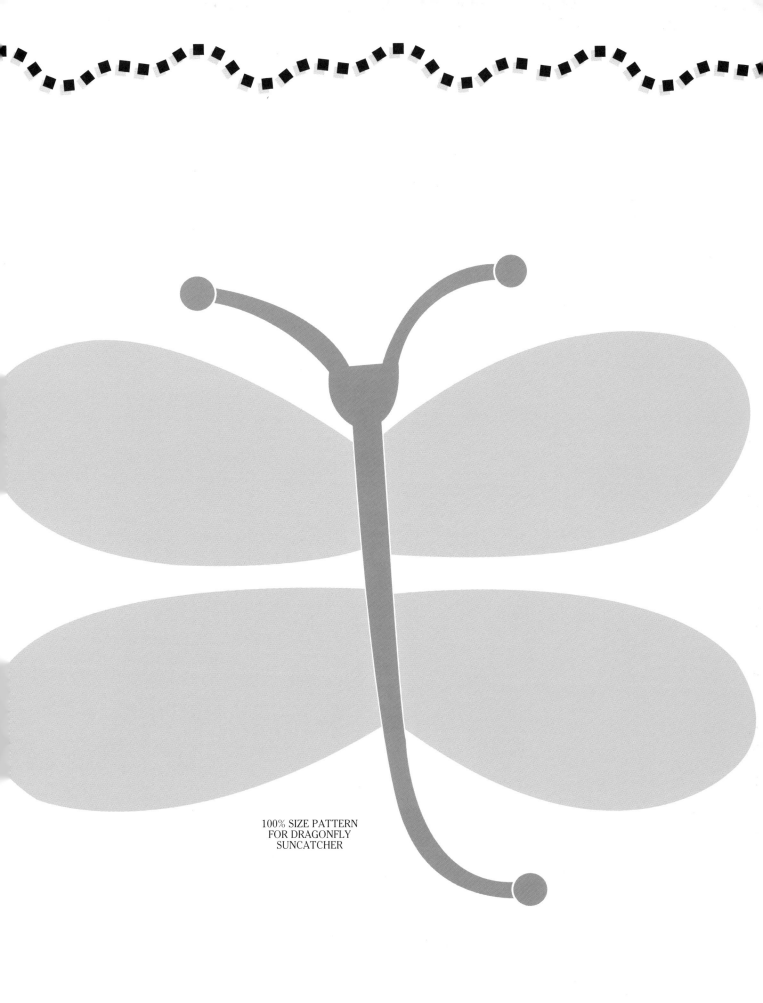

100% SIZE PATTERN
FOR DRAGONFLY
SUNCATCHER

100% SIZE PATTERN
FOR GECKO
SUNCATCHER

100% SIZE PATTERN
FOR BUTTERFLY
SUNCATCHER

Dragonflies rest on a golden vase that is a bright and elegant addition to your decor.

Candlelight sparkles through this votive alive with fluttering dragonflies.

Dragonfly Vase

by Heather McDonald

THE BEADERY® MATERIALS:
• 1 package each of Tiger Coral, Light Tiger Coral, Tortoise, Violet and Jade mosaic pieces • Package of Terra-cotta grout

MATERIALS:
Crisa 7" x 4" glass vase • Silicone sealer

Dragonfly Votive

by Heather McDonald

THE BEADERY® MATERIALS:
• 1 package each of Violet, Tiger Coral, Light Tiger Coral, Tortoise and Jade mosaic pieces • Package of Terra-cotta grout

MATERIALS:
3½" clear glass votive holder • Silicone sealer

PATTERN FOR VASE
AND VOTIVE
(100% SIZE FOR VASE)
(75% SIZE FOR VOTIVE)

Window Hanging

by Heather McDonald

THE BEADERY® MATERIALS:
• 1 package each of Tiger Coral, Tortoise, Light Tiger Coral, Jade, Violet and Alabaster mosaic pieces • Package of Terra-cotta grout

MATERIALS:
6" x 22" wood frame • 6" x 22" piece of clear plexiglass • Silicone sealer

Place on fold.

50% SIZE PATTERN
FOR WINDOW HANGING
(ENLARGE 200%)

Hang this bright design in your window for the look of stained glass. Sunlight will set the colors dancing.

Time marches on in colorful style when the clock is covered with this wonderful mosaic design.

100% SIZE PATTERN
FOR TOP OF CLOCK

Mantel Clock

by Heather McDonald

THE BEADERY® MATERIALS:
• 1 package each of Tiger Coral, Light Tiger Coral, Jade, Violet and Alabaster mosaic pieces • 2 packages of Terra-cotta grout
MATERIALS:
Provo Craft 9" x 8" mantel clock kit
• Silicone sealer
DIRECTIONS:
Flip clock face pattern for top of clock face.

100% SIZE
PATTERN FOR
FACE OF CLOCK

Sugar & Creamer

by Mimi Huszer Fagnant

THE BEADERY® MATERIALS:
• 1 package each of Alabaster, Light Tiger Coral, Jade and Rose mosaic pieces • Package of Ivory grout

MATERIALS:
Anchor Hocking glass sugar and creamer set
• Silicone sealer

Handcrafted table accessories add a touch of class to your table.

Bring a happy note to tea time with flower patterned servers.

100% SIZE
PATTERN
FOR SUGAR

Napkin Holder & Rings

by Mimi Huszer Fagnant

THE BEADERY® MATERIALS:
• 1 package each of Alabaster, Light Tiger Coral, Jade and Rose mosaic pieces • Package of Ivory grout

MATERIALS: 5" x 6" wood napkin holder • Wood napkin rings • Silicone sealer • White craft paint
Note: Basecoat wooden pieces with white craft paint

100% SIZE PATTERN
FOR NAPKIN RING

100% SIZE
PATTERN
FOR CREAMER

100% SIZE
PATTERN
FOR NAPKIN HOLDER

A big bowl of fruit makes this tray a joy to use and a delight to display.

Fruit Bowl Tray

by Mimi Huszer Fagnant

THE BEADERY® MATERIALS:
• 1 package each of Jade, Tiger Coral, Light Rose, Light Tiger Coral, Rose and Violet mosaic pieces • 2 packages of Alabaster mosaic pieces • Package of Ivory grout
MATERIALS:
Wood tray with 9" x 6" opening • Silicone sealer • White craft paint
DIRECTIONS:
Base coat wood with one coat of white craft paint.
Follow picture for placement of tiles.

100% SIZE PATTERN
FOR FRUIT BOWL TRAY

Yellow pears on a covered canister.
What a happy note to add to any kitchen!

Cherries bring a splash of color and cheer to your cooking day.

Pear Canister

by Mimi Huszer Fagnant

THE BEADERY® MATERIALS:
• 1 package each of Alabaster, Light Tiger Coral, Jade and Light Rose mosaic pieces • Package of Ivory grout
MATERIALS:
Provo Craft 9" canister •
Silicone sealer
DIRECTIONS:
Follow picture for placement of tiles.

Cherry Canister

by Mimi Huszer Fagnant

THE BEADERY® MATERIALS:
• 1 package each of Alabaster, Light Tiger Coral, Jade and Light Rose mosaic pieces • Package of Ivory grout
MATERIALS:
Provo Craft canister • Silicone sealer
DIRECTIONS:
Follow picture for placement of tiles.

100% SIZE PATTERN
FOR CHERRY CANISTER

100% SIZE PATTERN
FOR PEAR CANISTER

Goldfish swim in a sea of colorful mosaics. This bowl will add a Mediterranean touch to your sideboard.

Fish Fruit Bowl

by Lorraine Kazan

THE BEADERY® MATERIALS:
• 1 package each of Teal, Light Teal, Tiger Coral and Light Tiger Coral mosaic pieces • Package of Pewter grout

MATERIALS:
8½" x 3½" terra cotta bowl • Silicone sealer

DIRECTIONS:
Do fish patterns first, then place Teal and Light Teal tiles randomly around body of bowl.

100% SIZE PATTERN
FOR FISH FRUIT BOWL

Sky...Land...Sea.
This screen brings
nature indoors with
glowing beauty.

Top left image.

Top right image.

Second left image
(Reverse for second right image).

Third left image
(Reverse for third right image).

Fourth left image.

Fourth right image.

Folding Screen
by Lorraine Kazan

THE BEADERY® MATERIALS:
• 5 packages of Alabaster • 3 packages each of Dk. Teal and Jade • 2 packages of Lt. Teal
• 1 package each of Dk. Violet, Lt. Violet, Cobalt, Tiger Coral, Lt. Tiger Coral, Tortoise
• 3 packages of Pewter grout
MATERIALS:
2 panel photo screen • Ten 8½" x 10½" pieces of ⅛" plexiglass • 3 tubes of silicone sealer

25% SIZE PATTERNS
FOR FOLDING SCREEN
(ENLARGE PATTERNS 400%)

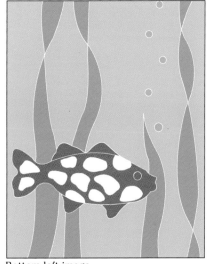

Bottom left image.

Bottom right image.

Seashells and Color. This vase will make a lovely addition to your home or a gift that will be received with pleasure.

Sea Life Vase

by Lorraine Kazan

THE BEADERY® MATERIALS:
• 1 package each of Alabaster, Teal, Violet, Jade, Light Teal, Tiger Coral, and Light Tiger Coral mosaic pieces • Package of Pewter grout

MATERIALS:
Crisa 13" Spring Valley vase • 3 packages of assorted small seashells • 2 tubes of silicone sealer

DIRECTIONS:
Randomly place Teal and Light Teal for water and Alabaster for sand on background, and randomly place Tiger Coral and Light Tiger Coral on starfish as shown.

Glue shells
here

50% SIZE PATTERNS
FOR SEA LIFE VASE
(ENLARGE PATTERNS 200%)

Glue shells here

Miniature Chest

by Mimi Huszer Fagnant

THE BEADERY® MATERIALS:
• 6 packages of Alabaster • 1 package each of Rose, Light Rose, Light Teal, Teal and Jade • 2 packages of White grout
MATERIALS:
Wood doll armoire • Silicone sealer

Left door pattern - flop for right door

Patterns for top front and top sides

75% SIZE PATTERNS FOR CHEST (ENLARGE PATTERNS 125%)

Pattern for bottom sides

Drawer front pattern

A little cabinet becomes
a work of art with
delicate mosaic flowers,
leaves and insects.

This delicate treasure casts a pearly, golden glow. Add it to any room to bring warmth and cheer.

Turtles have never been so appealing. This little creature is sure to inspire comment and laughter.

Turtle

by Heather McDonald

THE BEADERY® MATERIALS:
• 1 package each of Light Tiger Coral, Tiger Coral, Tortoise and Jade mosaic pieces • Package of Terra-cotta grout
MATERIALS:
7" x 10" ceramic turtle • Silicone sealer

Little Lamp

by Mimi Huszer Fagnant

THE BEADERY® MATERIALS:
• 1 package each of Teal, Violet, Jade and Rose mosaic pieces
• 2 packages of Light Tiger Coral mosaic pieces • Package of Ivory grout
MATERIALS:
Provo Craft White frosted glass lamp • Silicone sealer
DIRECTIONS:
Randomly place tile colors on lamp base. Use Light Tiger Coral on background of lampshade.